Ms. Hoenig

KALEIDOSCOPE

THE CALIFORNIA GOLD RUSH

by
Edward F. Dolan

BENCHMARK **B**OOKS

MARSHALL CAVENDISH
NEW YORK

Benchmark Books
Marshall Cavendish Corporation
99 White Plains Road
Tarrytown, NY 10591
www.marshallcavendish.com

Copyright © 2003 by Marshall Cavendish Corporation
All rights reserved.

Library of Congress Cataloging-in-Publication Data

Dolan, Edward F., 1924-
   The California Gold Rush / by Edward F. Dolan.
      p. cm. -- (Kaleidoscope)
Summary: Explores the phenomenon of the California Gold Rush, including
information about the routes to California taken by hopeful miners and
the fate of John Sutter, owner of the land on which gold was first
discovered.
Includes bibliographical references and index.
  ISBN 0-7614-1456-8
  1. California—Gold discoveries—Juvenile literature. 2. Frontier and pioneer life—California—Juvenile literature. 3. California—History—1846-1850—Juvenile literature. [1.California—Gold discoveries. 2. Frontier and pioneer life—California. 3. California—History—1846-1850.] I. Title. II. Kaleidoscope
(Tarrytown, N.Y.)
  F865 .D64 2003
  979.4'04--dc21
                              2002003947

Photo Research by Anne Burns Images

Cover photo by North Wind Pictures

The photographs in this book are obtained with permission and through the
courtesy of: *North Wind Pictures*: p.1(title),6,17,18,22,25,38; *The Granger Collection*: 5,10,13,14,21,26,30,33,34,37,42; Corbis: 9,29 Bettman; *Getty Images*: 41 Hulton Archive

Printed in Italy
6 5 4 3 2 1

CONTENTS

THE MAGNIFICENT DISCOVERY	4
THE FIRST NEWS	11
OVERLAND TO CALIFORNIA	15
BY SEA TO CALIFORNIA	20
IN THE GOLD FIELDS	27
THE FATE OF JOHN SUTTER	36
TIMELINE	44
FIND OUT MORE	46
INDEX	48

THE MAGNIFICENT DISCOVERY

It was raining hard on the morning of January 24, 1848. John Agustus Sutter was working in his office at his trading post when James Marshall—one of his best workers—strode in. Water poured from Marshall's clothing, but his face glowed with excitement.

Marshall's hands trembled as he pulled a small leather pouch from inside his coat and opened it. Instantly, Sutter understood the reason for the man's excitement. Out of the bag fell bits of a glittering yellow metal—gold!

In this magazine illustration, a miner leaps with joy, holding giant gold nuggets high, and shouts, "Eureka!" The Greek work, which means "I have found it!" has long served as California's state motto, in memory of the gold rush.

The Pilgrim rejoiceth over his "Pile."

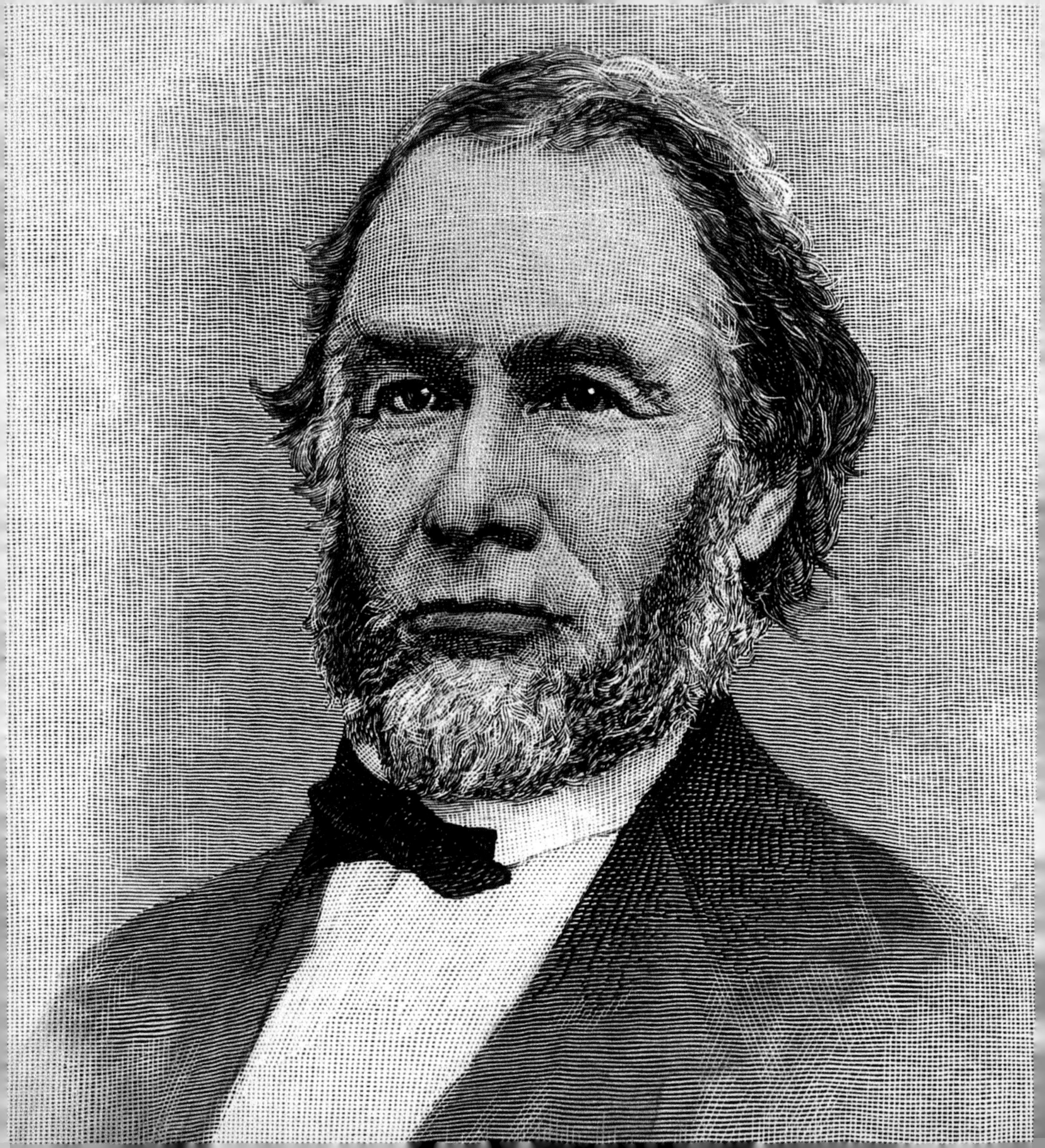

Marshall had been in charge of a crew building a sawmill for Sutter in the foothills of the Sierra Nevada, a nearby mountain range, for the last few days. There, in the waterway at the mill, he had glimpsed the yellow metal and filled the pouch for his employer to see.

The discovery left the German-born Sutter breathless. After leaving his native land in 1835, he had worked in parts of the United States and Hawaii. He settled in northern California four years later, in 1839, and quickly became a wealthy man. Then, thanks to his close relations with the Mexican government, he had been granted almost fifty thousand acres of land that spread across the Sacramento Valley and up into the Sierra Nevada.

James Marshall was the man whose discovery started the 1849 gold rush. Gold had actually been sighted several times before in California, but a flood of gold seekers was not triggered until word of Marshall's find reached the outside world.

On a portion of his land near the village of Sacramento, Sutter had built a trading post that was now famous throughout the United States as "Sutter's Fort." With its stores and workshops, it had become a major stopping place for the wagon trains that brought a growing number of settlers westward each year.

The fort had made Sutter a wealthy man. Now the discovery of gold on his property might make him one of the richest men on earth.

Or so he thought. Mexico had just been defeated in a war with the United States, and was about to surrender California as a result. Sutter was soon to lose his lands to the hordes of gold seekers who would now come flooding in to California from all over the world.

Gold was discovered here, at the mill James Marshall was building for his employer, John Sutter.

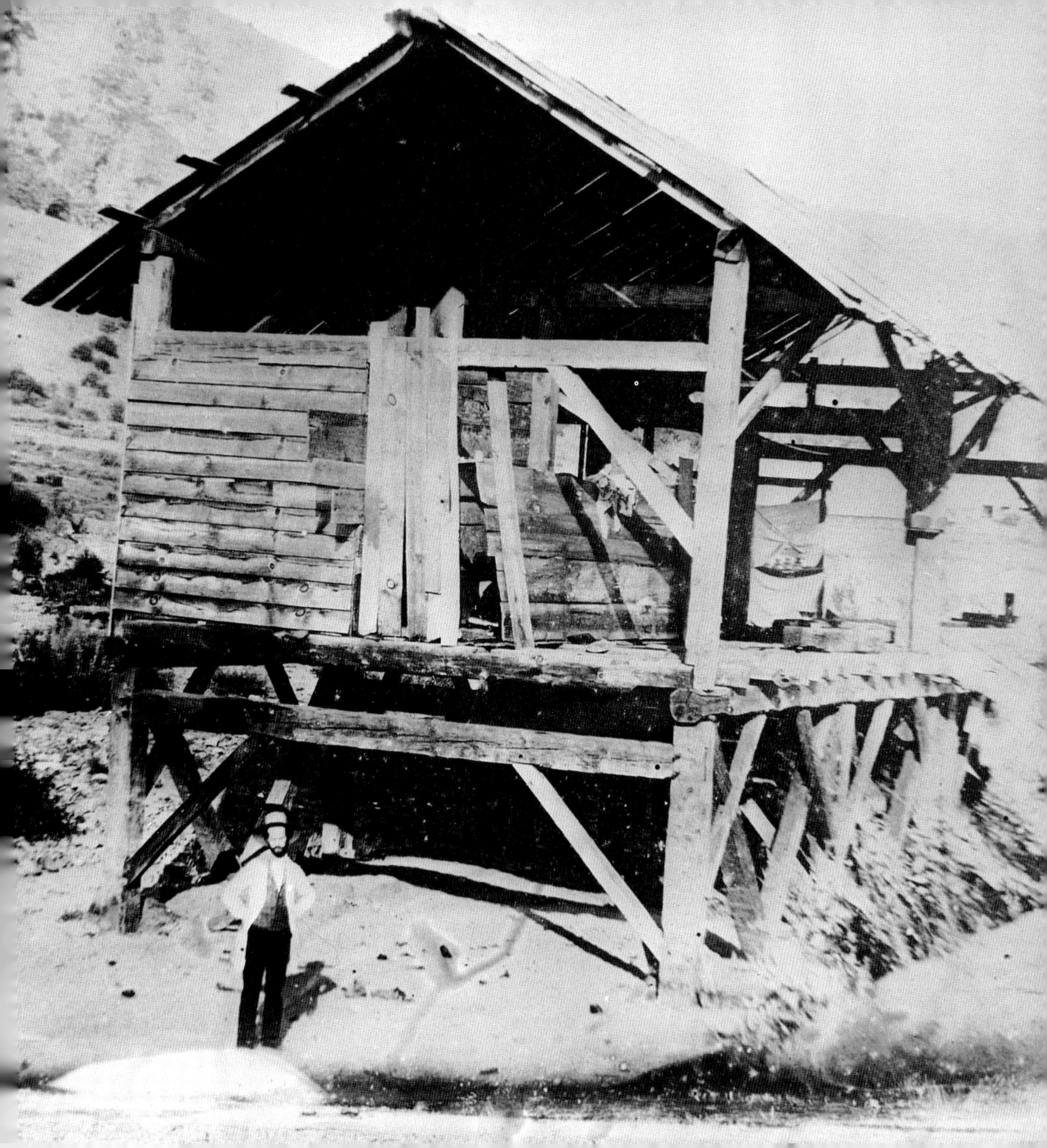

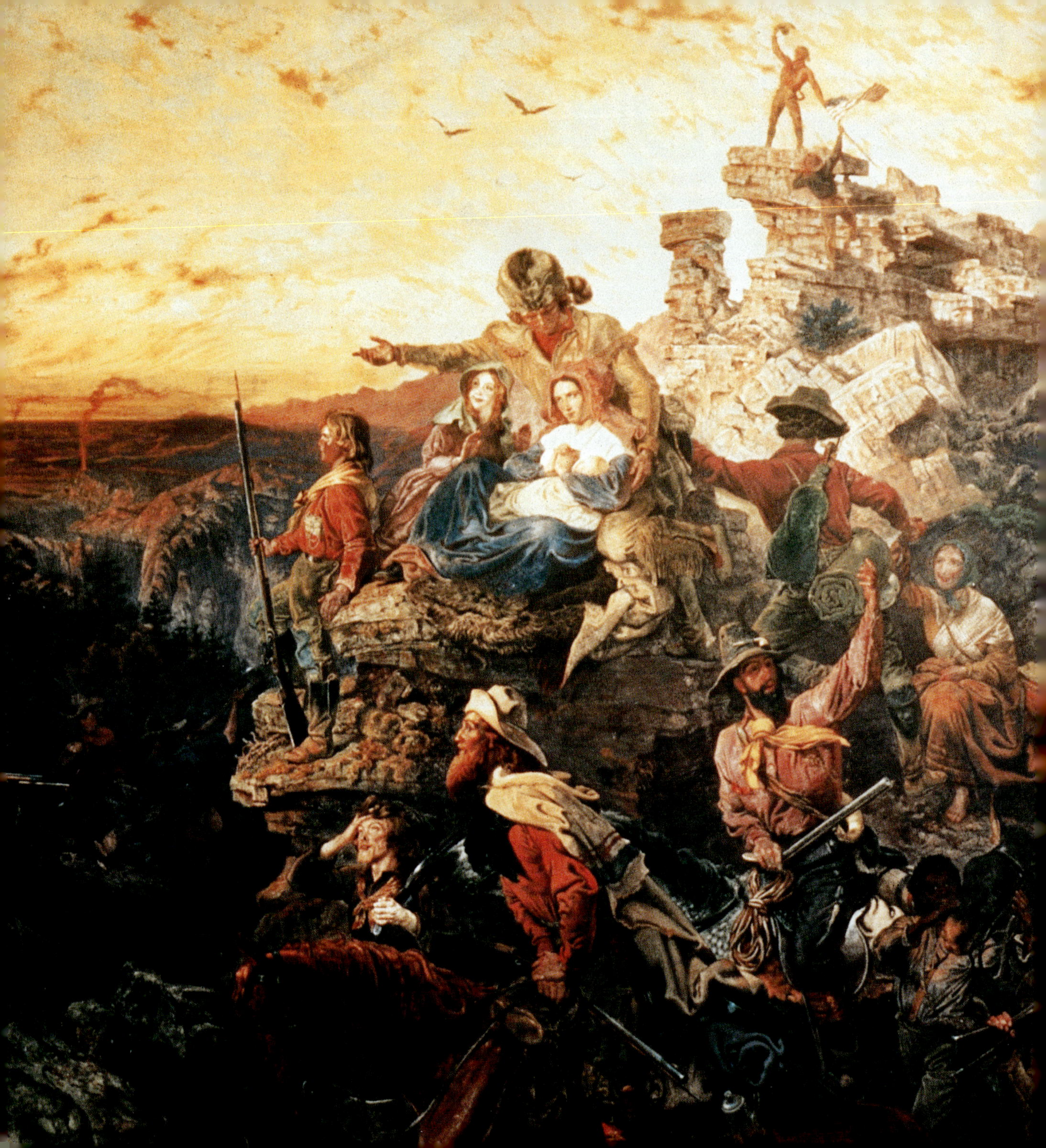

THE FIRST NEWS

When word of the discovery first began spreading out from Sutter's Fort, it failed to excite most Californians. They knew that gold had been found in earlier times and had earned little profit for anyone who went looking for it.

Finally, in mid-1849, word of this newest strike spread beyond California. It made its way into the nation's greatest newspapers. From there, it traveled across the world, bringing with it the news that the United States government had tested samples of the gold and found them to be of the highest grade.

This painting symbolizes the vast movement to the West in the mid-1800s. Gold did much to start the migration, though many families traveled west not in search of the precious metal, but to farm or start stores or other businesses.

Suddenly, thousands of people—not only in the United States, but everywhere—were bitten by "gold fever." It was a disease that triggered a wild rush to the West Coast of the United States. In 1849 alone, eighty-thousand gold seekers hurried to northern California and into the Sierra Nevada foothills. They were nicknamed "the forty-niners," and were soon followed by thousands more.

A wagon train carrying settlers and hopeful gold miners makes its way west along the Sweetwater River in Wyoming. Before ending its journey in California, the train would pass through rich farmlands and arid deserts, go around the Great Salt Lake, and cross the towering Rocky Mountains and Sierra Nevada.

13

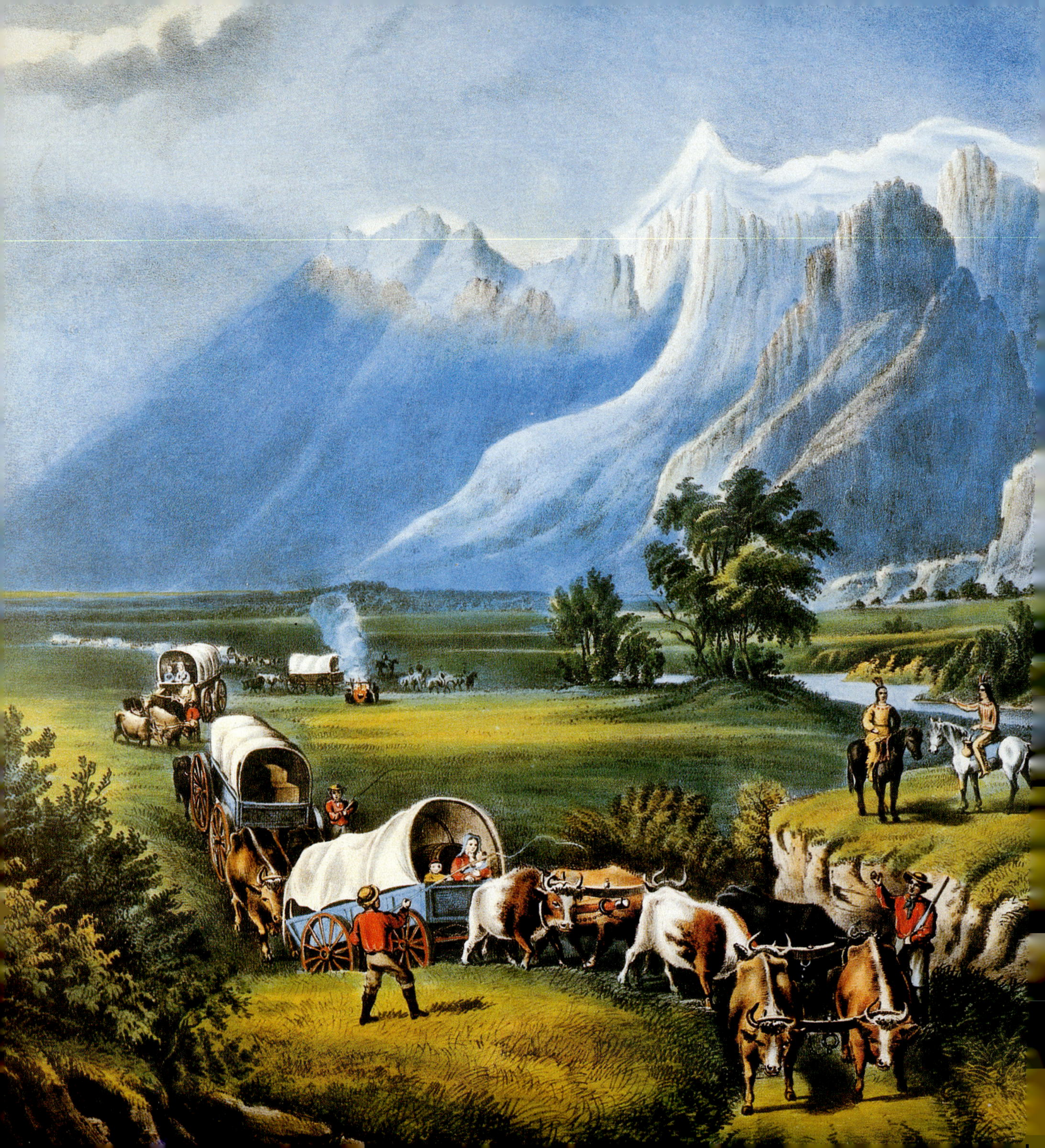

OVERLAND TO CALIFORNIA

Those thousands traveled to California by any of three routes—one overland and two by sea. The greatest number, several hundred thousand in all, chose the overland route. They headed west in wagon trains from a string of towns along the Missouri River, among them St. Joseph, Missouri; Council Bluffs, Iowa; and Omaha, Nebraska.

The journey began on trains that brought hopeful settlers to the start of the Oregon Trail. The travelers followed the trail across the Midwestern plains to the Rocky Mountains. There, they cut through South Pass,

In this 1866 lithograph, a westbound wagon train leaves the Rocky Mountains behind after crossing South Pass in Wyoming.

15

a gently rising opening that made its way between the towering peaks of the Rockies.

The travelers then reached another roadway—the California Trail. They swung their wagons onto it and headed southwest toward the goldfields. They left behind the Oregon Trail, which continued on to the northwest region of the United States.

The trail west held constant dangers for the travelers. The hazards ranged from Indian attacks, starvation, and illnesses to wild, rushing rivers and trails on which wagons could easily overturn.

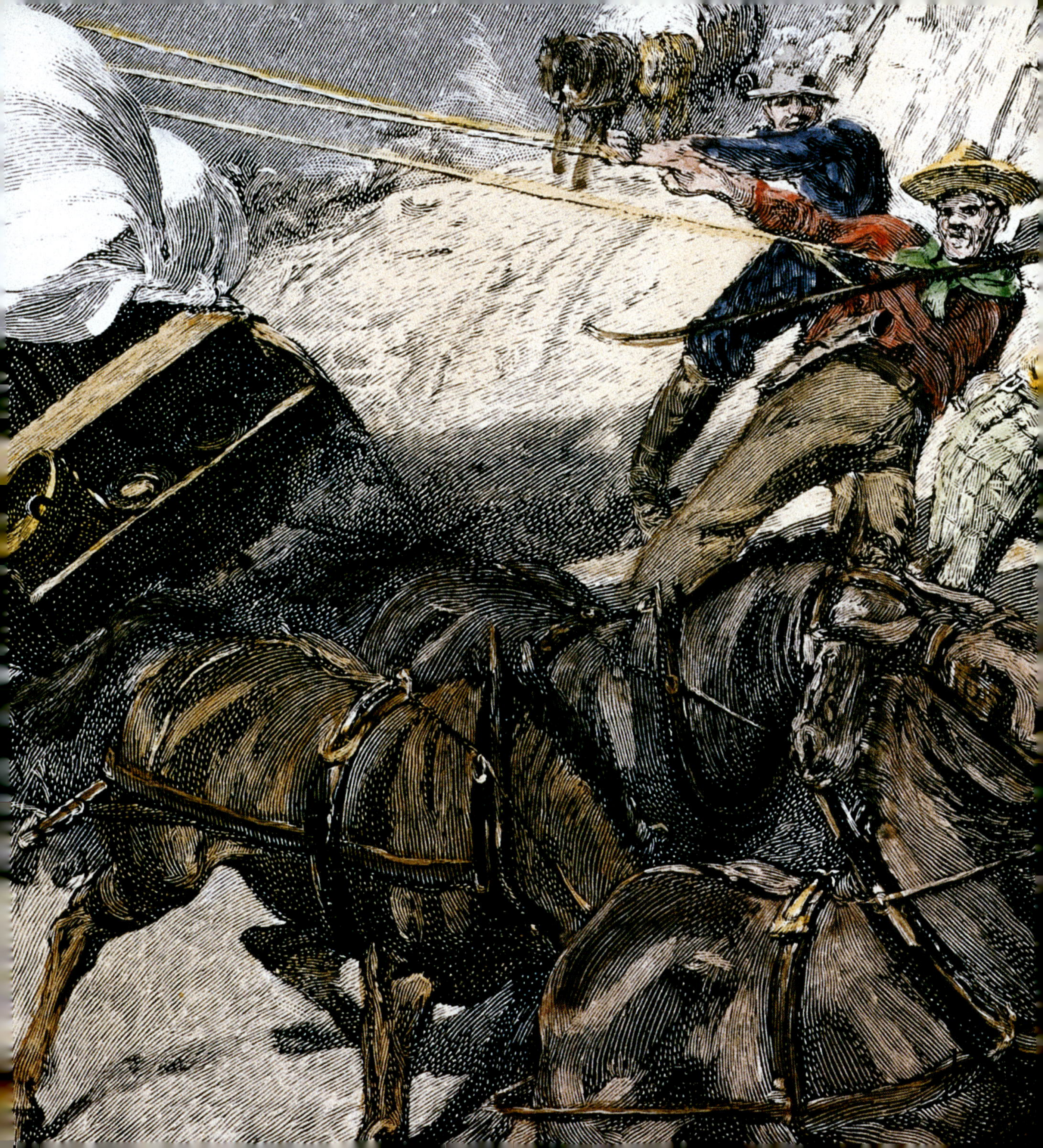

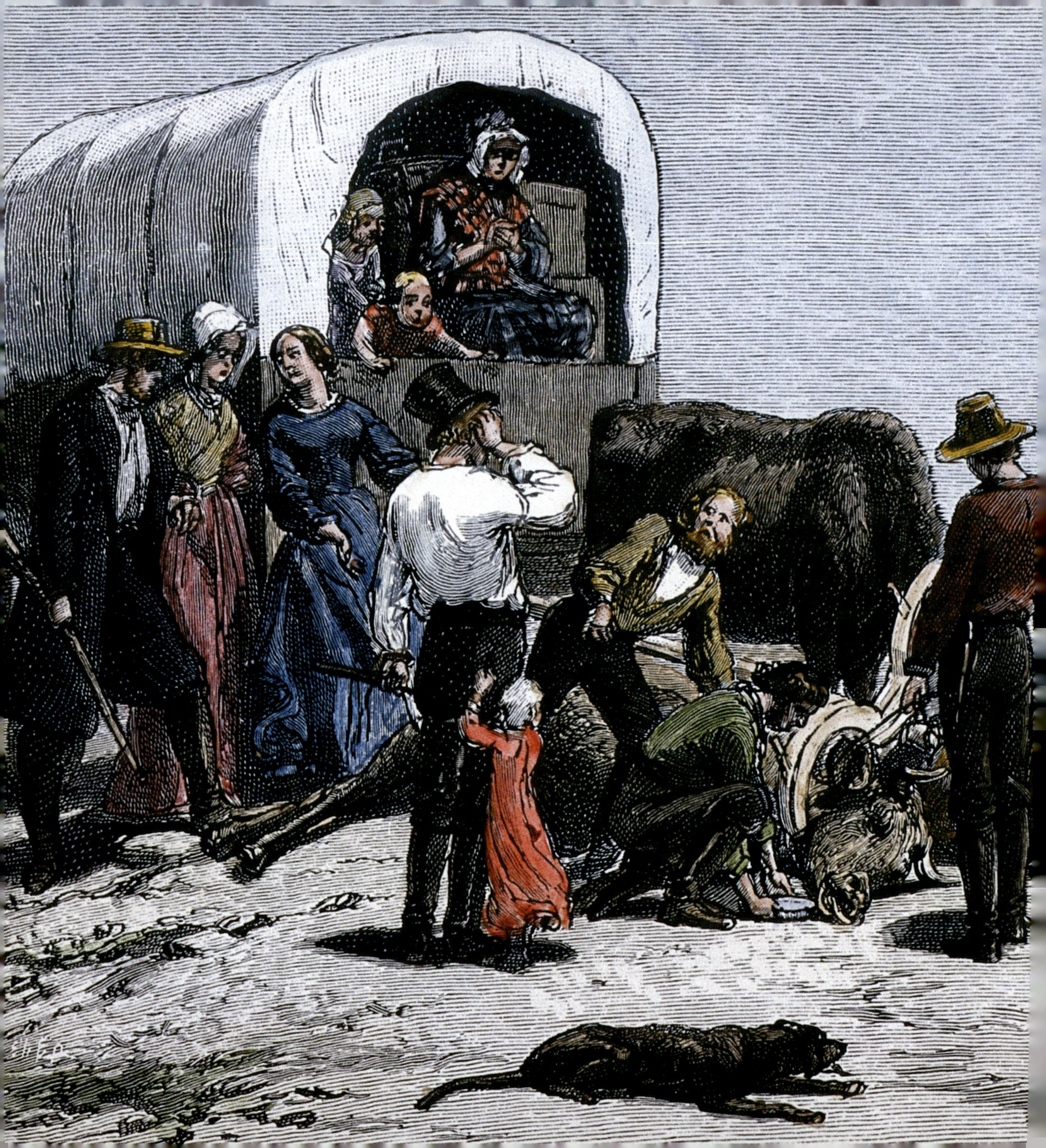

Soon, the California-bound wagons were struggling through Utah's blistering heat. Pushing on for 500 miles (800 kilometers), they reached the eastern slopes of the Sierra Nevada. Then up and over the towering peaks they traveled, finally descending to the fertile fields of California.

Part of the route to California made its way through arid deserts. Often, the oxen pulling the pioneer wagons dropped dead of thirst on the trail.

BY SEA TO CALIFORNIA

More than 100,000 gold seekers made their way to California by sea. They chose one of two routes to reach their destination. In both cases, they first sailed down the Atlantic Ocean from one of a number of East Coast cities. Then, on reaching the Caribbean Sea, they separated into two groups.

One group continued to the foot of South America, and then pressed westward through the wildest water in the world to reach the Pacific Ocean. From there, they sailed northward until they reached the California port of San Francisco.

This poster from the gold rush era advertises a route to California by sea. Though vessels of all types sailed to the Pacific Coast, this company featured clipper ships. Famous for their speed, they were given their name because they moved along at "a good clip."

Coleman's California Line,
FOR SAN FRANCISCO,
SAILING REGULARLY AS ADVERTISED

Clipper of SATURDAY, March 17th.

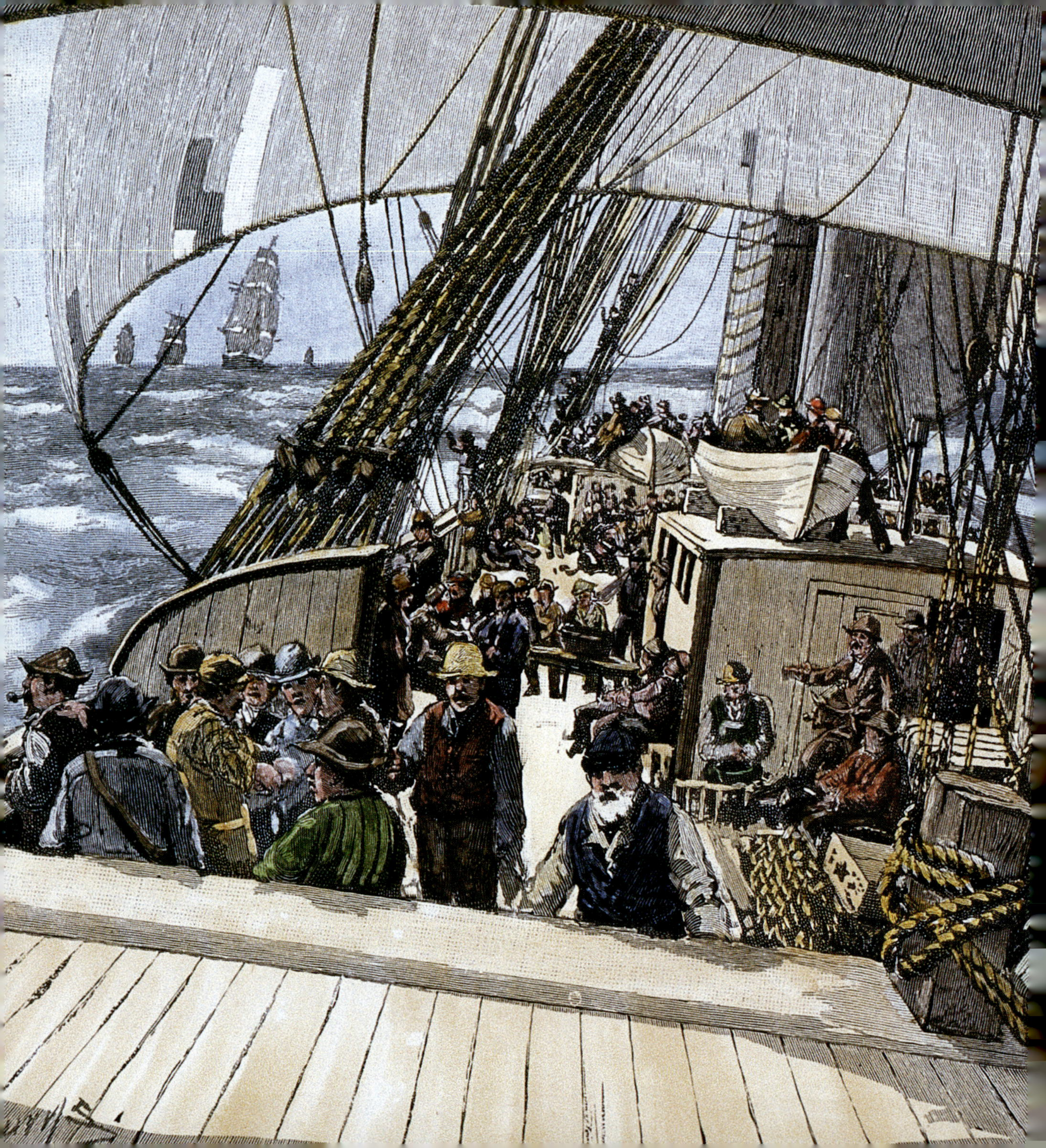

The journey cost each traveler between $300 and $500 dollars (approximately between $7,000 and $11,000 U.S. dollars today!). It lasted for some 6 months and covered about 13,000 miles (21,000 kilometers).

Those wanting a shorter trip boarded ships that carried them across the Gulf of Mexico and dropped them on the eastern side of the Isthmus of Panama. Then, traveling in turn by foot, canoe, and mule train, they crossed the isthmus. All the while, they struggled through thick jungles alive with alligators, snakes, giant spiders, and wild birds.

California-bound gold seekers are pictured enjoying fine weather on this ship cutting across the Gulf of Mexico toward the Isthmus of Panama. After reaching Panama, they would still face a difficult hike through forty miles of jungle to the Pacific Coast.

Their trek brought them to the beaches along the western side of Panama. There, they camped until they could board passing ships for the final run to San Francisco. The journey usually took three months to complete. It cost about the same as the trip down around the foot of South America. Both sea routes were extremely dangerous and many travelers lost their lives before ever reaching California's goldfields.

As difficult as the hike across Panama was, travelers who chose to sail from the Atlantic Ocean to the Pacific via the foot of South America faced even greater dangers. The winds and storms that developed in South America are among the worst in the world, and they sent a number of the sailing vessels to the bottom of the ocean.

25

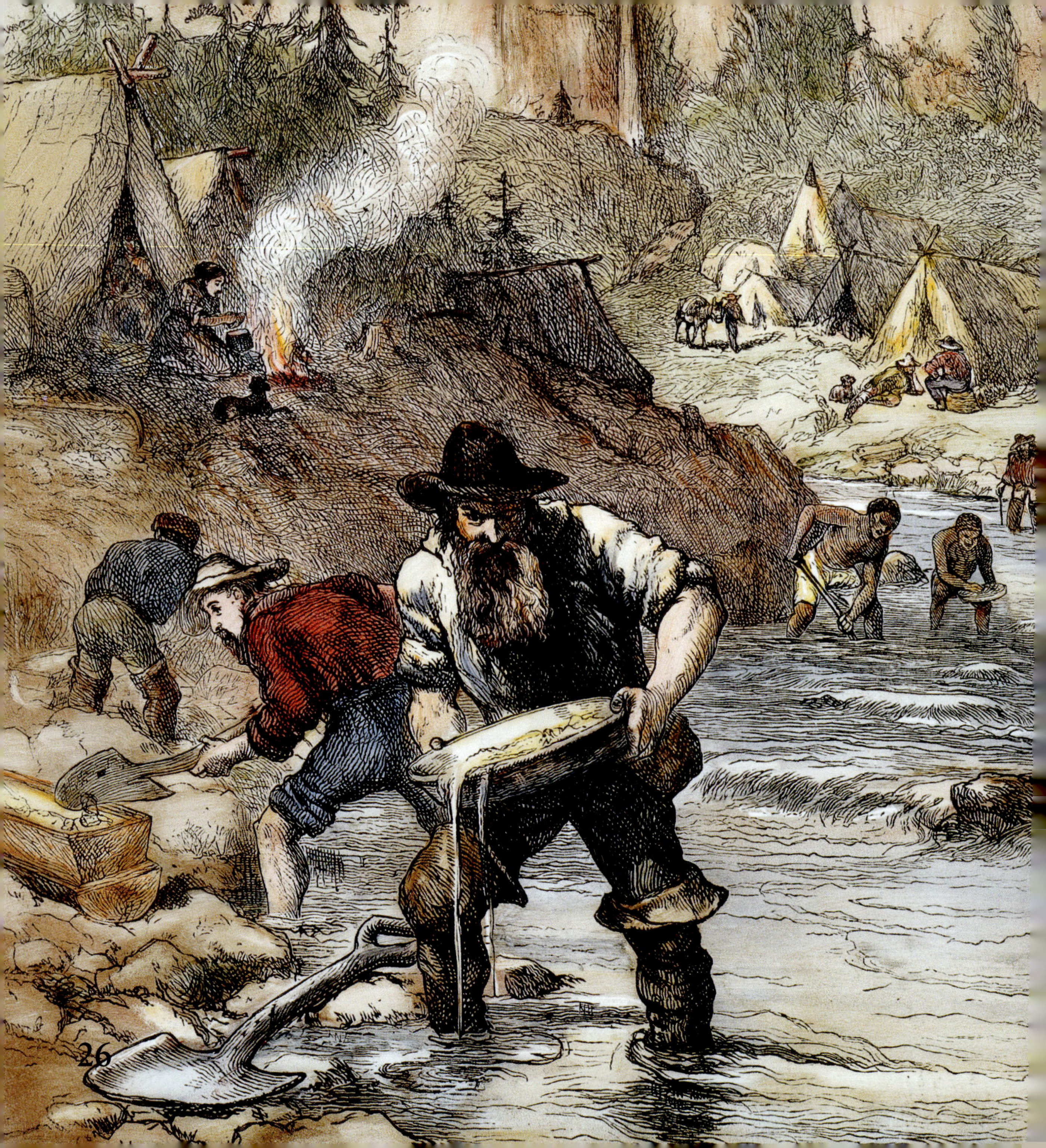

IN THE GOLDFIELDS

Whether they arrived by wagon or ship—and no matter whether they came from the eastern United States, the British Isles, mainland Europe, China, or Australia—the newcomers quickly made their way to the Sierra Nevada Mountains. There, they crouched in icy streams, filled metal pans with sand from the bottoms, and hoped to see the sparkle of yellow bits in them. In their quest, they founded mining camps in an area about 200 miles (322 kilometers). They gave the camps some of the most unusual names in American history, among them Rough and Ready, Sucker Flat, Red Dog, and You Bet.

In this engraving, the miners pan for gold in a fast-moving Sierra Nevada stream. Each man filled his metal pan with sand from the bottom, drained away the water, and hoped that sparkling bits of gold would be left behind.

Many of the camps were abandoned when the nearby gold ran out. But many survived to become modern cities. For example, today's Placerville and Nevada City are former mining camps. Placerville was originally called Hangtown, while Nevada City was known as Deer Creek Diggings.

Nevada City is pictured in this early photograph. Sitting at the foot of Sugar Loaf Mountain, it is now a modern city.

UNION LIVERY STABLE

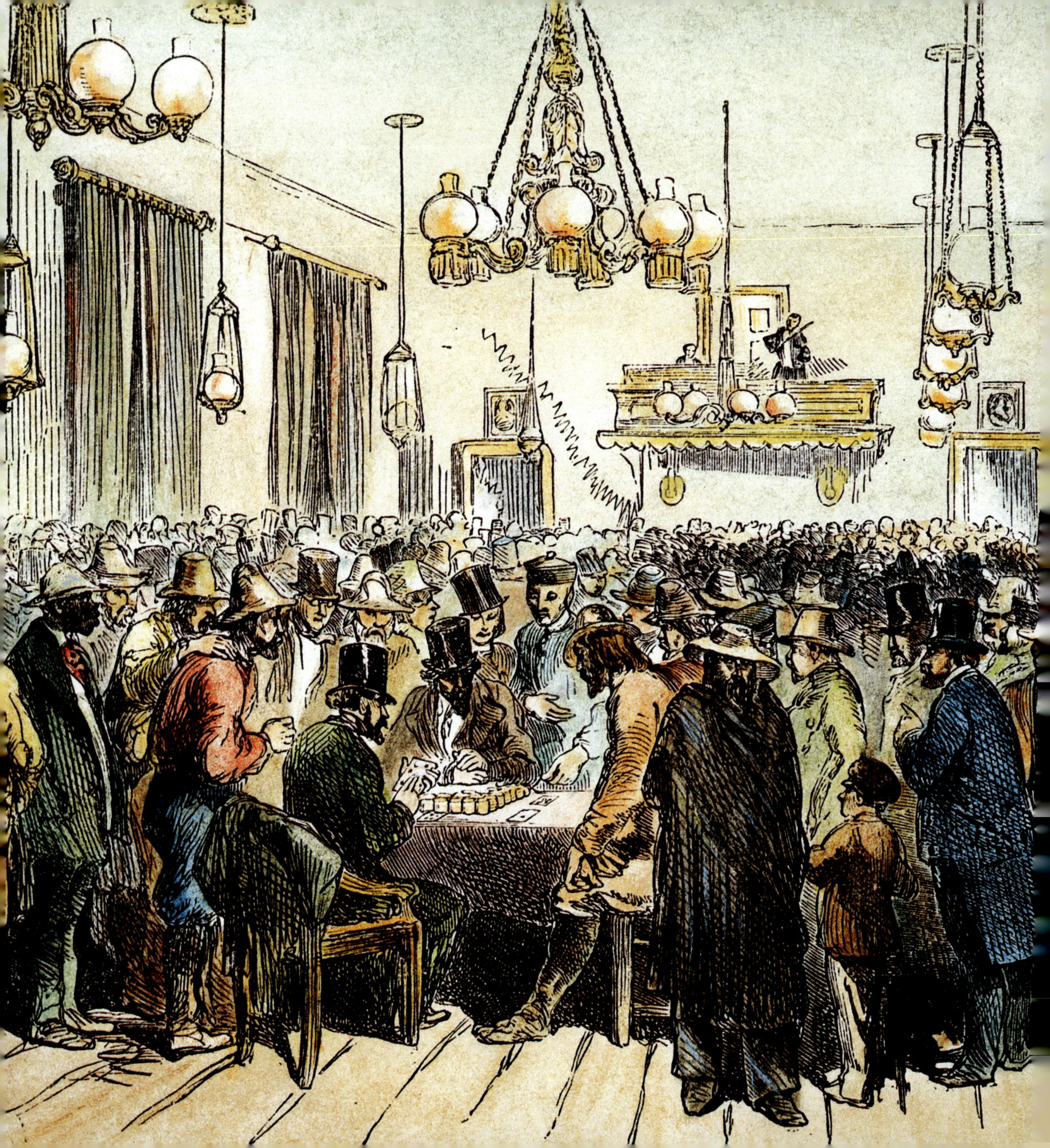

Life was wild in the camps, with the gold seekers sharply divided into two groups. Most were honest men in search of wealth for their families, but all around them were criminals—from crooked gamblers to outright thieves—out to snatch that wealth away. The honest and the dishonest were constantly clashing, usually in the saloons and gambling halls that sprung up in every camp. The problems ranged from brawls and gunfights to knifings and murders.

Most gambling halls in the goldfields were smaller than the one pictured here. Some were housed in tents, and others were little more than wooden shacks. But the same cannot be said of this one, the El Dorado gambling hall in Sacramento. It was well lit and featured a balcony for an orchestra.

Most miners did not make the fortunes they sought. Some lost all their gold nuggets and dust in the gambling casinos, or in crooked card games with professional cheats. Some, lonesome for their families, returned home after finding a few dollars' worth of gold. Some decided to forget about quick riches. They started businesses or began to farm the fine California soil. In either case, they brought their families west.

Only a few miners made fortunes in the goldfields, but many remained in California when the gold rush ended. They were joined by thousands of others who were lured west by posters promising a healthful climate and fine land for farming.

CALIFORNIA
The Cornucopia of the World

ROOM FOR MILLIONS OF IMMIGRANTS

43,795,000 ACRES OF **GOVERNMENT LANDS** UNTAKEN

Railroad & Private Land for a Million Farmers

A Climate for Health & Wealth without Cyclones or Blizzards

34

A number of men made great fortunes without ever visiting the goldfields. Among them were Charles Crocker, Mark Hopkins, Collis Huntington, and Leland Stanford. They became wealthy by selling farm and mining supplies to the newcomers, and then, in the 1860s, they went on to build the nation's first transcontinental railroad. It connected the Pacific Coast with the eastern half of the nation.

Equally famous was the merchant Levi Strauss. After arriving in 1853, he joined a friend in manufacturing heavy denim trousers that became favorites in the goldfields. Called blue jeans, they featured copper rivets that kept the pockets from tearing loose when heavy weights, such as gold, were placed in them.

Pictured here are some of the people Levi Strauss employed to manufacture his blue jeans. The employees are standing in front of the main Strauss office in San Francisco.

THE FATE OF JOHN SUTTER

While these men achieved great success in the gold rush, the same cannot be said for John Sutter. He lost his property to the flood of newcomers. At first, the gold seekers passed through on their way to the Sierra Nevada. But then, on failing to become rich, many returned and began surrounding his fort with farms. At the same time, the city of Sacramento was taking shape nearby. It was soon crowded with stores that ruined Sutter by selling the same goods that he had sold for so long.

As a young man, John Sutter came to northern California, where he built his large trading post.

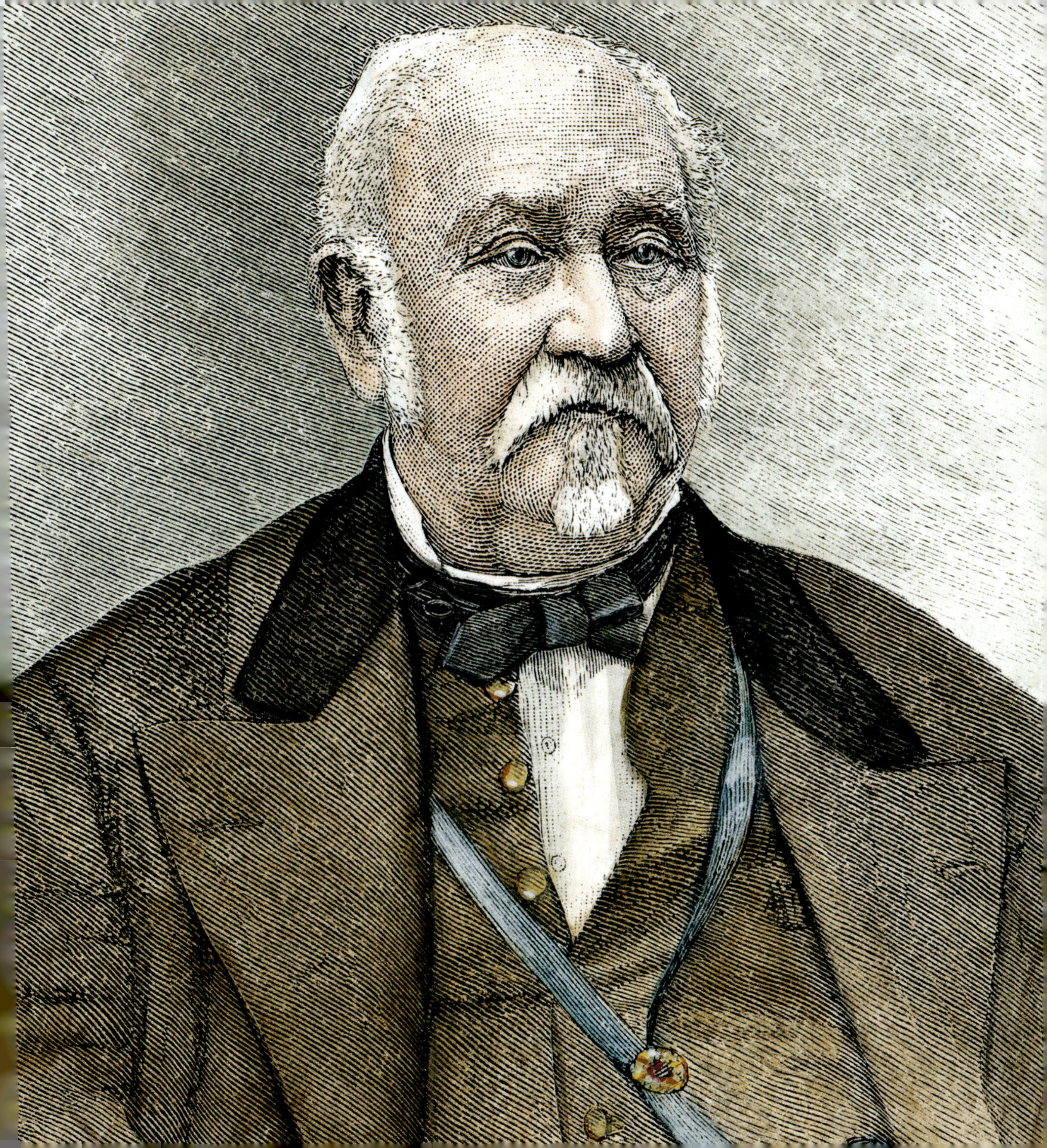

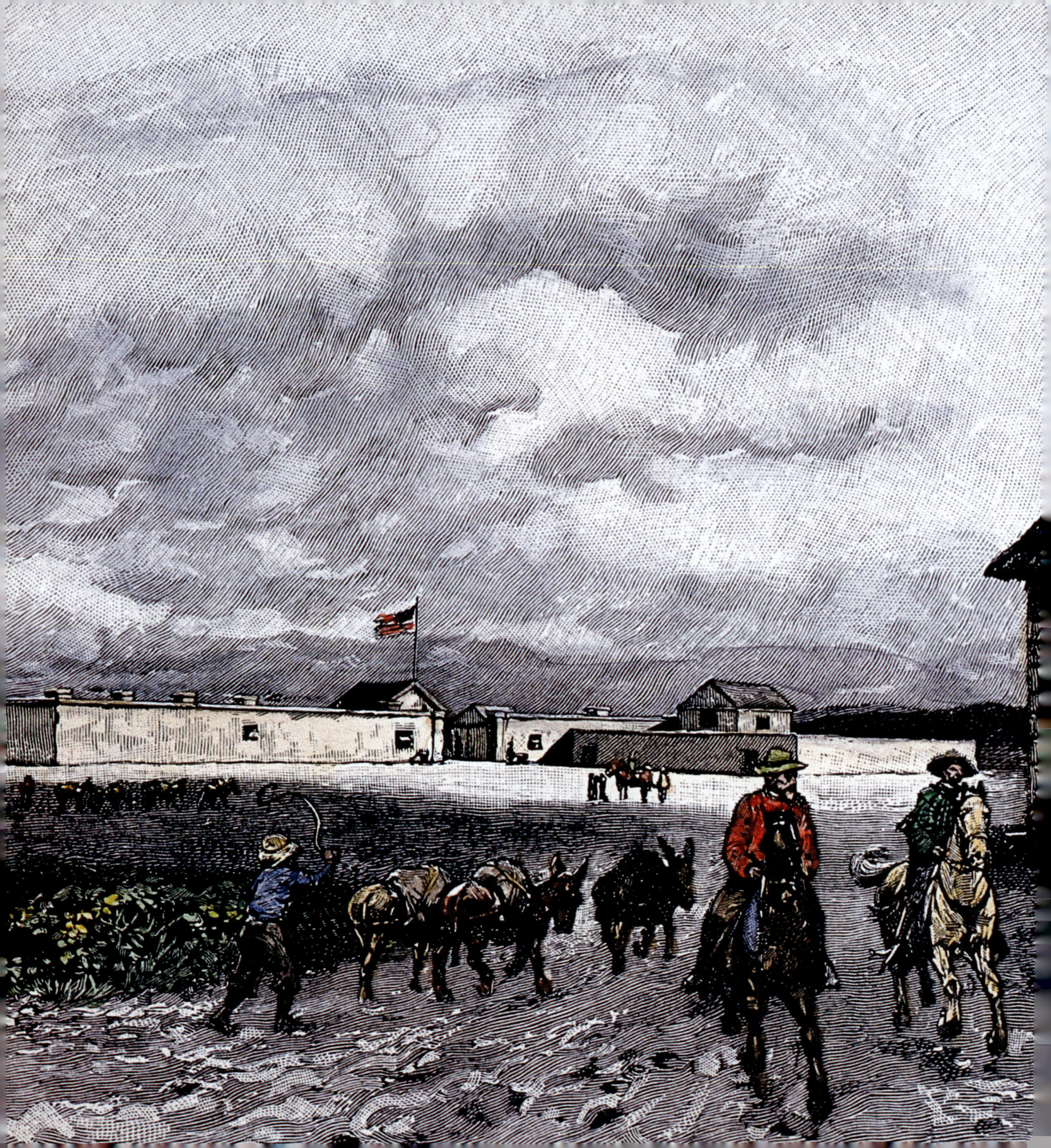

Within two years of the start of the gold rush, Sutter was penniless. Powerless to keep his acreage safe from outsiders, he saw his stores, blacksmith forge, repair shops, and storerooms go out of business. His orchards, fields, and animals vanished when farms began popping up all around him.

He struggled vainly for years to have the U.S. government pay him for his lost land. Government leaders were reluctant to help him, however, because his land had come to him from Mexico. His struggle finally ended in 1880 with his death at age seventy-five.

This engraving shows Sutter's Fort in Sacramento as it looked in the 1840s. It stands today near the city's downtown area and the grounds of California's state capitol.

The gold rush had begun to fade by 1852. But its end did not signal the end of gold mining in the state. Rather than individual miners who panned the streambeds, companies that used hydraulic mining began to extract gold commercially. They used water forced through high-pressure hoses and nozzles to separate the gold from the earth surrounding it.

Commercial gold mining remained a major business in California until the 1860s. Farming eventually replaced it as the number one industry.

The gold rush drew men and women to America's West Coast from all over the world. Among them were the Chinese workers seen here. Many Chinese also went into business, as the owners of restaurants, small hotels, and laundries.

41

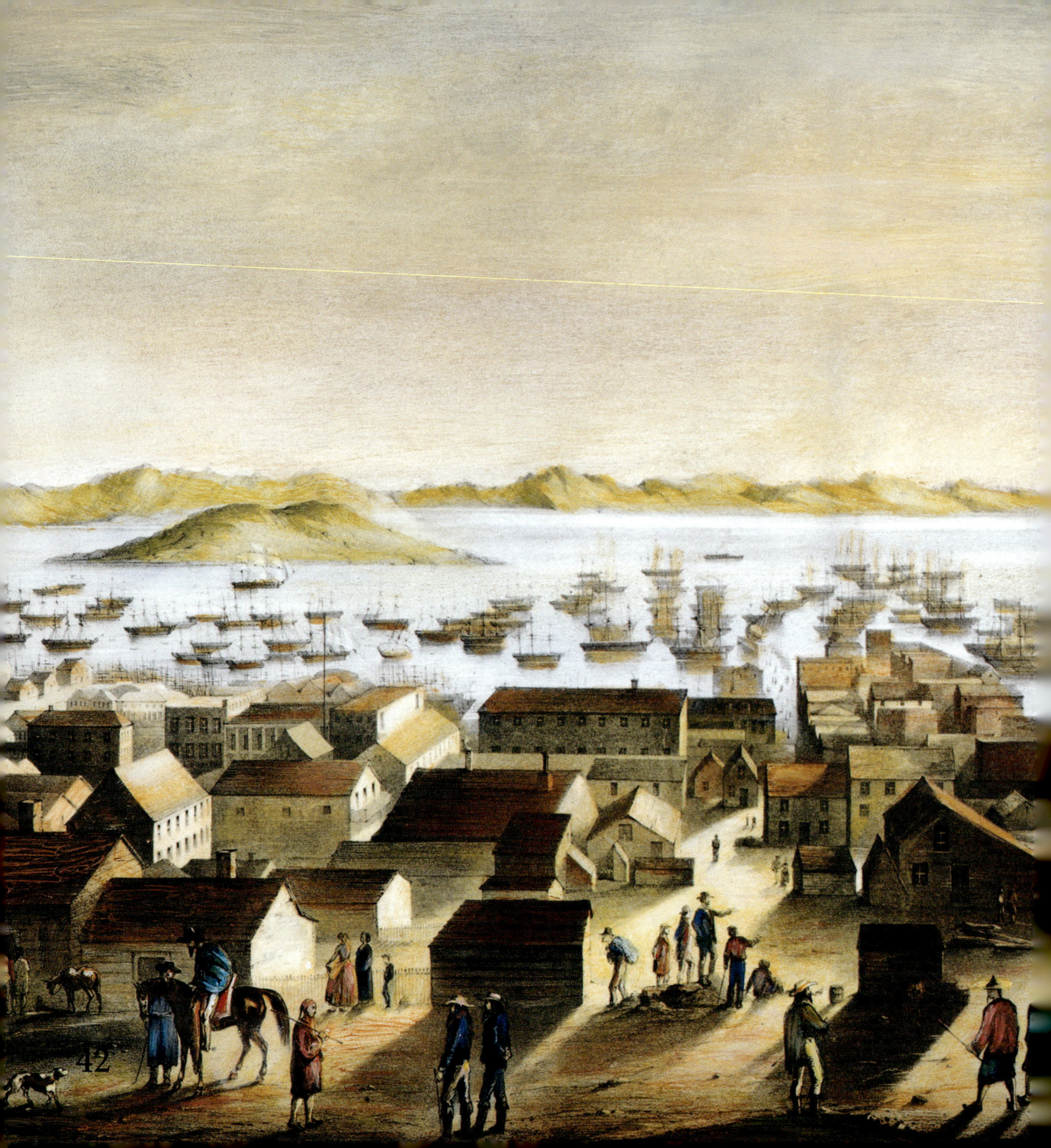

The gold rush was a thing of the past by then. But left behind was the undying memory of one of the nation's most exciting and valuable moments, a moment in history that contributed so much to the growth of the American West.

The city of San Francisco as it looked in the 1850s. Anchored in the Bay are many of the ships that carried the miners westward and then had no way of returning home—because their crews ran off to the goldfields.

TIMELINE

1839 John Sutter arrives in California. He will befriend officials of the Mexican government, receive a land grant of 48,818 acres, and build his famous trading post.

1848 In late January, while building a sawmill for Sutter, James Marshall sights bits of gold on his employer's property in the foothills of the Sierra Nevada. A week later, on February 2, California is transferred to the United States by the Mexican government. The transfer follows a successful takeover of the region by the American army and navy.

1849 News of the gold strike reaches the outside world and triggers a rush to California from the eastern United States and a number of foreign countries. As a gateway to the goldfields in the Sierra Nevada, the small village of San Francisco starts on the road to becoming a major city. Its population of eight hundred people quickly balloons into the thousands.

1850 California is admitted into the Union as the nation's thirty-first state on September 9. John Sutter is left penniless after losing his land to an army of newcomers. His future efforts to have the United States government reimburse him for his lost acres will fail. He will die in 1880.

1852 The gold rush begins to wind down. However, commercial goldmining remains California's major enterprise until being replaced by agriculture in the 1860s.

FIND OUT MORE

BOOKS

Blake, Arthur, and Pamela Dailey. *The Gold Rush of 1849: Staking a Claim in California.* Brookfield, CT: Millbrook Press, 1995.

Brinkley, Douglas. *American Heritage History of the United States.* New York: Viking, 1989.

Dolan, Edward F. *Famous Builders of California.* New York: Dodd Mead, 1987.

Holliday, J.S. *Rush for Riches: Gold Fever and the Making of California.* Berkeley, California: Oakland Museum of California and University of California, 1999.

Zollinger, J. Peter. *Sutter: The Man and His Empire.* Gloucester, MA: P. Smith, 1967.

WEBSITES

California's Untold Stories: Gold Rush!
Oakland Museum of California
www.museumca.org/goldrush/

The American Experience
Wayback: The Gold Rush
www.pbs.org/wgbh/amex/kids/goldrush/

AUTHOR'S BIO

Edward F. Dolan is the author of more then one hundred nonfiction books for young people and adults. He has written on medicine and science, law, history, folklore, and current social issues. Mr. Dolan is a native Californian, born in the San Francisco region and raised in Southern California. In addition to writing books, he has been a newspaper reporter and a magazine editor. He currently lives in the northern part of the state.

INDEX

Page numbers for illustrations are in boldface.

blue jeans, 35
businesses, **9**, 32, **34**, 35, 36, 39, 40

California, 4, 44, 45
California trail, 16
Chinese, 27, **41**
costs, 23, 24
Crocker, Charles, 35

dangers, **17**, 19, 23–24, **25**, 31

farming, 32, **33**, 39, 40
forty-niners, 12, 31–32, 35

gambling, **30**, 31–32
gold fever, 12
gold rush
  early strikes, 4–11, **9**
  end, 40, 45

Hopkins, Mark, 35
Huntington, Collis, 35

Marshall, James, 4–7, **6**
Mexico, 8, 44
mining, 40
mining camps, 27–31, **29**, **30**

Oregon Trail, **14**, 15–16

panning, **26**
pioneers, **10**, **13**, **14**
posters, **21**, **33**

railroad, 35
routes
  land, 12, 15–19
  sea, 20–24, **21**, **22**, **25**

Sacramento, 36, **38**

San Francisco, **42**, 45
Sierra Nevada, **26**, 27
Stanford, Leland, 35
Strauss, Levi, **34**, 35
Sutter, John, 4–8, 36–39, **37**, 44, 45
Sutter's Fort, 8, **9**, **38**

timeline, 44–45
transportation, **13**, **14**, 15–23, **18**, **21**, 35

wealth, 11, 32, 35
websites, 46

48